LARRY
BURKETT

WILLS &
TRUSTS

MOODY PRESS
CHICAGO

ISBN: 0-8024-2610-7

1 3 5 7 9 10 8 6 4 2

Printed in the United States of America

About the Author

Larry Burkett is committed to teaching God's people His principles for managing money. Unfortunately, money management is one area often neglected by Christians, and it is a major cause of conflict and disruption in both business and family life.

For more than two decades Larry has counseled and taught God's principles for finance across the country. As president of Christian Financial Concepts, Larry has counseled, conducted seminars, and written numerous books on the subject of maintaining control of the budget. In addition he is heard on more than 1,000 radio outlets worldwide.

SECTION I
Guidelines
for Inheritance

STEWARDSHIP GUIDELINES

Even a brief survey of the Bible reveals that God provided for each generation through inheritance. In biblical times, the sons inherited their fathers' properties and thus provided for the rest of their family.

What is not so obvious, in most instances, is that the sons received their inheritance while their fathers were still living. Thus, a father was able to oversee their stewardship while they were learning. It would be interesting to see what money management training most children would receive if their parents knew they would turn over all the estate to them and depend upon them for their support.

I challenge every Christian to develop a godly approach to inheritance beginning right now. It is important to establish some fundamental absolutes about your inheritance.

1. Training for wife. Ensure that the wife understands how to handle money well. If a woman has never actually managed money, this training starts with basic budgeting. Both the husband and wife should go through Christian Financial Concepts' course on family financial planning. After completing this course, the wife should actually manage the home finances for at least the next year.

2. Create wills/trusts. Every living American should have the basic legal document for after-death asset distribution—a will. Some families will need a "trust" to manage their assets in order to reduce estate costs and/or save taxes. There are many varieties of trusts and, contrary to most opinions, their use is not limited to large estates.

3. Develop a plan. In addition to the legal instruments necessary to distribute and manage your estate, you must have a plan. For instance, at what age do you want to begin your children's training? How much will you entrust to their management? Who will help advise them?

Obviously each family's plan will be different, but the one common factor for Christians should be an understanding of God's principles for managing money.

THE IMPORTANCE OF HAVING A WILL

The making of a will is a simple, straightforward, businesslike way of handling your affairs. It can be an expression of gratitude to God and to others for the goodness you have received in this life, and can relieve others of unnecessary grief and mental anguish because things have "been prepared in advance of the need."

Failure to have a will is to neglect the God-given opportunity provided for you to direct, in writing, the disposition of your real and personal property at the time of your death. Failure to have a will is also to neglect the opportunity to appoint a guardian for your children, if you and your spouse die at the same time. When there is no will, your family can be caused needless inconvenience, costly delay, and additional expense. To die intestate (without a will) is to allow your state to draft your will for you! You might not agree with the decisions of your state regarding your property, your furnishings, and, most of all, your children's destiny, but you can do very little about it if you die without a will. The law makes no provision for stewardship; nor does it provide for the option of the appointment of a special guardian for your minor children, unless previously specified in a written will.

GOD'S WILL AND YOUR WILL

Stewardship, for the Christian, is more than just being accountable for tithes and offerings given to the Lord's work. It is also the accountability for what happens to your resources in the future. You should honor God through your estate. All that you have you hold in trust from the Lord. As good stewards of this sacred trust, you should give careful consideration to the final distribution of your possessions with a proper expression of Christian gratitude, which can be done through having a will. Is God's will included in your will? Remember what God's Word says in 2 Corinthians 5:10 about appearing before the Lord one day and giving an account of your stewardship.

SECTION II
Questions About Wills

Perhaps the best way to discuss this issue is in a question-and-answer format. This will help you to understand what kind of estate planning is best for your family.

Is it really necessary to make a will?

Most people, Christians included, don't like to discuss death, so they delay talking about it until it's too late. And if they die without a will, no one, including their spouses, can make one for them.

The state will decide how the assets of the decedent (deceased person) are distributed, which may be totally contrary to what he or she would have chosen. Thus, if you want things done your way, make a will as soon as possible, because none of us knows what the future holds.

If both parents were killed at the same time, the state would appoint a guardian for any minor children. This guardian would actually raise the children and decide where they would go to church and school, where they would live, and the type of medical care they would receive. Thus, having your choice of guardian is reason enough to make a will.

A widow with two small children may have to divide an estate three ways, with one-third going to her and two-thirds going to the children. Even though she is the children's guardian, the widow may need to get permission from the court before spending the children's portion. In addition, she may need to explain expenditures to the court and furnish a detailed accounting on a regular basis.

Hardship may also result for elderly parents or loved ones who are handicapped if the person responsible for supporting them dies without a will. The decedent may have objected to his or her loved ones being placed in an institution, but that could happen if the decision is left to the state.

One final word about dying intestate. Some couples argue that they don't need a will because all their possessions are in joint ownership with right of survivorship. True, joint ownership with right of survivorship will transfer property to the surviving spouse automatically at the death of the first spouse; but if both spouses die at the same time, there's no surviving joint owner to inherit the property. Without a will, its distribution will be decided by the state.

Aren't wills just for large estates?

Mention an estate and most people will probably think of huge, elaborate homes with maids, butlers, and well-manicured lawns, but according to the law, you have an estate whether large or small. Your estate consists of everything you own. Cars, furniture, antiques, savings accounts, and even books are considered part of your estate. And many people have a larger estate than they realize when they add up things like retirement and life insurance benefits and their homes.

A common argument against wills is "I don't need one; I'm not worth enough." That is poor stewardship of what God has entrusted to a Christian.

What are the requirements for preparing a will?

In order to be valid, a will must meet the legal requirements of the state where the decedent lived. The process of determining a will's validity is called probate, which actually means to prove, or to testify. Legal requirements for valid wills may vary from state to state, but in general, you should have a will prepared in the state in which you live.

It's a good idea to review your will on a regular basis—some suggest once a year. Ask your attorney if there are new federal or state laws that would require your will to be updated.

Do I need a new will if I change residences from one state to another?

Possibly. You need to have an attorney in the new state review your will to ensure it conforms to that state's laws.

Where is the best place to store my will?

In order to probate a will, the original copy must be delivered to the court. For that reason, the original copy should be kept in a safe location, such as your attorney's office or with other important papers you have.

A note in your home files should indicate where the original copy is stored. It's also good to keep a copy of the will yourself for future reference.

Many people place their original wills in a safe-deposit box. Depending on the state you live in, your bank officer may be allowed to enter the box after your death and search for your will.

Other states may have more strict guidelines for entering safe-deposit boxes. If you live in one of those states, you may need to authorize another person to enter the box. Otherwise, a court order may be needed to enter it, which could create unnecessary delays in the probate process. Furthermore, if no one knows about the safe-deposit box, it might be impossible to find the will.

I'm a "do-it-yourself" person when it comes to things around the home. Is it also possible for me to do my own will?

A question often asked is, "Can I do my own will, or do I need an attorney?" The law allows a person to draft his or her own will. One example is a *Holographic Will*, which is done entirely in the handwriting of the person who made it.

However, if you draft your own will, you're increasing the risk of its being contested or declared invalid. What's worse is that, if you do it wrong, it's too late to correct it after you die.

Will kits, which may cost as little as $19.95, are another option for preparing your own will. For some people, these kits are excellent—particularly if the estate is small and the kit uses computer software to generate the will. In this case, the will could be printed out, which reduces the possibility of errors. But the use of will kits should be limited to those who know exactly what they want. Remember, a flaw in the will could invalidate the entire document.

If you have a simple estate situation and are willing to shop around a little, you can probably find an attorney who will draft your will for a modest fee.

I need to change a will I made several years ago. Does this mean I have to do an entirely new will?

Because you never know what may happen ten or twenty years in the future, it's possible that changing circumstances could require an update of your will. If this occurs, it is not necessary to make an entirely new will.

Instead, these changes could be made through the use of a codicil, or supplement. The codicil is subject to the same laws of probate as the will, so it must be drafted properly, and only the "original" is valid in court. Attach all codicils to the original will and store them together. If you have previous wills in existence, you should specify that your latest will supersedes all previous wills.

What if one of my witnesses has died?

In order for a will to be probated, the judge may require the will to be verified. If you used only two witnesses and the state requires a minimum of two, both must be alive. It always is best to use three or even four witnesses that you know well. If less than the required minimum are still alive, you will need to amend your will with a codicil to have other witnesses verify it.

I'm in the process of preparing a will, but I'm very concerned about leaving money to two of my potential heirs. My son is involved with things I cannot support as a Christian, and my daughter can't seem to control her spending. What should I do?

Most people should be concerned about what happens to their property after death, especially if they're committed to being good stewards of what God has entrusted to them. If you share this concern, you may choose to withhold or regulate an inheritance if it is going to support an organization or lifestyle you do not condone. Such action might be necessary if one of your children is involved in a cult.

Remember that any assets you leave behind are not yours, but God's, and you need to exercise stewardship of those assets in the best possible way. In the case of a cult, would the Lord want the benefits of your estate to go to an organization that leads people away from His Son? It's quite possible a cult would demand a high percentage, or possibly all, of your child's inheritance.

By all means, you'd want to share with your children the reason you couldn't include them in your will. You'd also need to assure them that you still care very much for them and lift them up in prayer daily. Eventually, their resentment might be replaced with respect because of your faithfulness and the influence of God in your life.

In the case of a child who is a spendthrift or chronically unemployed, a parent might choose to regulate, rather than withhold, an inheritance. A trust could be set up to achieve this goal. The controlling trustee would be someone other than the child, and limits could be placed on how the trust funds were used.

I am concerned about how my heirs will use their inheritance in case of my premature death. They were not taught proper stewardship principles.

Parents of teenagers and young adults who weren't raised under the influence of God's principles of finance will have special challenges. Many times these parents were saved when they reached middle age, and the spending patterns of their children had been established already. And, often the children will not even be Christians. If you know your heirs

17

are not qualified to handle an inheritance with wisdom and discipline, then by all means prepare alternatives. Trust funds can be set up, with a Christian executor appointed who has the authority to determine whether or not funds should be made available for uses presented by the heir(s). Specific guidelines should be established, listing acceptable uses for the funds, such as starting a low-budget business, educational expenses, purchase of a residence, and the like. You will need a committed volunteer as executor, a cooperative banking institution, and an attorney experienced in the field of trusts. God expects us to be worthy stewards of all He has given us, and preparing a will is an important part of good stewardship.

How do I divide my assets fairly among my children?

Dividing your assets equally between your children, while taking into consideration their desires, is a difficult task but not an impossible one. It's wise to prepare for your eventual death and the disposal of your estate, but don't get so caught up in leaving material possessions that you overlook leaving a spiritual inheritance.

You might consider having all of your assets appraised by a qualified appraiser. Then ask each child to make a list of the items he or she wants in the order of desire. If two children select the same item as their first preference, and say both are men, then let them draw lots to see which one gets the item. If a brother and sister select the same item and it is a female item, then the sister ought to get it. After all items have been selected, adjustments should be made in cash. For instance, if the total value of your estate is $25,000 and you have five children, each child would be entitled to values totalling $5,000. When you die, the child who gets items valued at over $5,000 should pay the estate the difference, to be distributed to those children not receiving their $5,000 share. Since some items may be sold before or at your death to cover the expenses of your last illness, burial, and related expenses, this distribution may not be exactly the way each heir desires. However, you can rest in the assurance that you did all you could to divide your estate equitably.

My parents are creating divisions among their sons' families over parental desires to provide the children with an early inheritance. Even though they are Christians, they are trying in some ways to dictate terms on the use of the money.

Your parents have noble intentions of giving their children an early inheritance. In biblical times the sons inherited their fathers' properties and thus provided for the rest of their family. "A good man leaves an inheritance to his children's children and the wealth of the sinner is stored up for the righteous" (Proverbs 13:22). In most instances, the sons received their inheritance while their fathers were still living. Thus, a father was able to oversee their stewardship while they were alive. The parable of the prodigal son in Luke 15 reflects this principle. "House and wealth are an inheritance from fathers" (Proverbs 19:14).

However, the attitude of your parents toward money has created a threat to serving God. "For where your treasure is, there will your heart be also" (Matthew 6:21). Money can cause anxiety, worry, and family conflicts; it can corrupt Christians, tempt them to indulge, and build their egos. But money doesn't have to do any of those things if it is placed under God's control so He can direct its use.

Your parents need to seek professional counseling about their spiritual lives. Even though you mentioned that they are Christians, they apparently need spiritual guidance. You should sit down with them and encourage them to talk to their pastor or a Christian counselor. To prevent future family conflicts, you should discuss this openly and honestly and resolve it from the beginning. An issue as sensitive as this will eventually cause more complications. Genesis 2:24 says, "A man shall leave his father and his mother and shall cleave to his wife; and they shall become one flesh." Ephesians 5 instructs wives to honor their husbands even as they honor the Lord and husbands to love their wives and treat them as their partners in the Lord. In other words, husband and wife are ONE. Whatever she has belongs to him; whatever he has belongs to her. They must decide whether they believe what God says or whether they just say they believe. Many good marriages have been destroyed through a lack of trust. Couples need to reevaluate their marriages according to scriptural principles, which means they have a 100 percent commitment to each other and a 100 percent commitment to God.

If your parents persist in dividing the sons' families over this inheritance, you should commit this matter to prayer and ask God to mend their relationship with each other and with Him.

SECTION III
The Executor

I've been told that I need an executor for my will. Does it really matter who I appoint?

One of the most unfortunate errors associated with making a will is choosing the wrong executor. A common misconception is that the executor is simply a person with an important title but no power or authority. As a result, some believe the entire responsibility of settling an estate falls on the attorney. However, the reverse is true.

Some of the many duties of an executor include:

- Locating the will and studying it
- Conferring with the attorney who drew up the will
- Locating witnesses and notifying creditors

- Locating all the deceased person's property
- Obtaining all canceled checks for the past several years
- Inspecting real estate, leases, and mortgages
- Filing an income tax return for the deceased person
- Filing estate tax returns
- Preparing information for the final accounting, including all assets, income, and disbursements

How many executors do I need?

Often your spouse is the best selection for the position of executor. In the will, you would simply name your spouse as executor and he or she would name you.

It's also a good idea to name an alternate executor who can take over if the spouse can't serve. This alternate could be another family member, a CPA, or an attorney who's familiar with your circumstances and assets and knows where you keep important documents.

You could also elect a third alternate, such as a major bank with a trust or estate department. You would come under their fee schedule, but in return they would have an orderly way of administering estates.

If you don't name an executor in your will, or if the person you choose fails to serve and you have no alternates, then the court will appoint someone to fill the position. Before you name someone as executor, make sure you talk with him or her first to see if he or she is willing to accept all the responsibilities. It's also a good idea to stay in touch with your intended executor to be sure this person still willing and/or able to do the job.

Do I have to pay the executor?

Compensation for the executor is another issue that needs to be considered. If you and the executor agree that he or she will serve without compensation, you can request that in your will. You can also request that the executor serve without the usual required bond.

If you die without a will and the court appoints an executor for your estate, that individual could receive a percentage of your estate as compensation. In Georgia, for example, this percentage may be as high as 5 percent. However, the executor may choose to waive compensation if he or she so desires.

Considering all that my executor has to do after my death, is there anything I can do now to make his or her job easier?

No matter who you appoint as executor, you can make his or her job a lot easier by maintaining a detailed inventory of all your assets. (See the *Checklist of Important Documents* at the end of this book.) One of the executor's duties will be to locate your assets, and if you have a detailed inventory, it can reduce the time and trouble required to perform this service. As a result, you can save unnecessary expenses and delays in settling your estate.

SECTION IV
Inheritance Taxes

I've heard stories about people who lost a major portion of their estate to taxes. Is there any way to avoid the tax bite when making my will?

Your estate is potentially subject to federal or state taxes at your death, and depending on how you make your will, the state where you reside, and other factors, your tax burden can be very low or very high. However, a properly prepared will can significantly reduce and, in many cases, eliminate a potential tax burden.

Two types of inheritance taxes are levied against an estate at death: (1) federal estate taxes and (2) state death taxes. The impact of both can be tremendous, but the federal tax has the potential to claim a much larger portion of an estate.

Fortunately, there are ways to escape some, or even all, of the federal estate tax burden at the death of one's spouse. One of these ways is to prepare a simple will, in which the husband leaves everything to his wife and she leaves everything to him. As a result, their estate is qualified for the *Unlimited Marital Deduction*, which means the surviving spouse won't owe a penny of estate tax when the other spouse dies.

Regardless of how big your estate is, $100,000 or even $100 million, there is no estate tax on the first death if everything is left to the surviving spouse. This can result in tremendous savings, because estate tax can run as high as 55 percent of the fair market value of the estate.

The resulting financial burden can be so great that survivors must sell everything just to pay the tax, especially if illiquid assets—such as a family farm—are involved. The farm might not be a major income producer, but if it's located next to a major city, the land might be worth millions.

Owners of the farm might disagree with such an evaluation, but the amount of tax that must be paid is based on the "fair market value" of all the assets a person owns—not how much the owner thinks his property is worth.

Another provision that can be used to reduce the federal estate tax is the *Unified Credit*. This provision allows a person to make transfers during life or after death of up to $600,000 to people other than his or her spouse and pay no estate tax on that amount.

This is an excellent provision to use in leaving property to children, other relatives, or friends. If it's properly used by both spouses, the benefits can be doubled. For example, the husband and wife each have a $600,000 exemption. They can prepare their will in such a way that the two $600,000 units protect up to $1.2 million of the estate from estate taxes. The property can go outright to the children or into a trust for the benefit of the children and surviving spouse.

If it goes into a trust, the surviving spouse could have life income rights over the trust and a right to invade the principal of the trust for health, maintenance, and support. He or she could be given the maximum rights allowed by law over the trust property, yet the property could still qualify for the *Unified Credit*. At the death of the surviving spouse, the remaining property in the trust would go to the children.

In addition to the *Unified Credit*, the tax law provides for an *Annual Gift Tax Exclusion*, which allows you to give up to $10,000 per donee annually without being subject to the gift tax. For a couple, the tax-free amount is $20,000 per donee per year. Thus, a husband and wife with three children could gift up to $60,000 per year to their children with no gift tax consequences.

For people with large estates, these gifts are a means of reducing the estate's size, which reduces the assets that are potentially taxable. This can be very helpful to widows with large estates.

Are state death taxes a cause for concern when planning my estate?

Although the Federal Estate Tax Code exempts all assets left to a spouse and up to $600,000 left to other beneficiaries, the same is not necessarily true of state death taxes. Many states have adopted the same code as the federal government, but others have not. If you happen to live in one of the states that tax an inheritance, the financial shock can be severe.

In 1990 the tax on a $600,000 estate left to a spouse was **$36,000** in **Pennsylvania, $25,500** in **Massachusetts**, and **$17,050** in **Louisiana**. When estates are left to children, the tax impact can be even greater. Using the same 1990 figures, the tax on a $600,000 estate left to a child was **$56,250** in **Wisconsin, $45,370** in **Kentucky**, and **$41,250** in **South Dakota**.

Many couples have actually changed their state of primary residence to avoid these taxes. What's more, state death taxes are graduated and, as such, will increase as the estate grows.

How are state and federal taxes paid on an estate?

The amount of federal estate taxes and state death taxes can have a significant impact on heirs because the taxes must be paid in cash. As already mentioned, illiquid assets may have to be sold in order to raise enough money to pay the tax. And due to the urgency of the situation, heirs may have to settle for less than the real value of the assets.

For that reason, it's wise to arrange for estate liquidity during your lifetime. One option for achieving this goal is life insurance, but you must plan carefully so that insurance proceeds won't raise inheritance taxes and probate costs.

For example, in the case of a $500,000 life insurance policy, the proceeds might be subject to estate taxes, even though they would be free of income tax. As a result, half the policy value could be lost to estate taxes. This situation could be avoided by establishing an irrevocable trust to "own" the policy and provide income and principal benefits for the spouse and children.

These trusts can be set up in a number of ways, but the key result is that when the insured person dies, the insurance proceeds are not subject to estate tax. Because they are owned by an irrevocable trust, they are not part of the insured person's estate.

Do you feel it is scriptural to tithe on an inheritance?

Proverbs 3:9 says to "honor the Lord from your wealth and from the first-fruits of all your produce." An inheritance should be considered part of your "increase," a portion of which you can give back to the Lord to honor Him. Second Corinthians 9:6 states, "He who sows sparingly shall also reap sparingly; and he who sows bountifully shall also reap bountifully."

SECTION V
Questions About Trusts

S imply stated, a trust is a vehicle for owning and managing assets. You create a trust, transfer assets into it, and choose a trustee to manage the assets and disburse them to beneficiaries.

A trust can be "intervivos" (during life) or "testamentary" (at death). Just as the name implies, an intervivos trust is drafted and implemented during a person's lifetime. As a result, these trusts are also referred to as "Living Trusts." In contrast, a *Testamentary Trust* is set up to begin when a person dies.

A trust may also be "revocable" or "irrevocable." If it is revocable, the trustor (trust maker) reserves the right to modify or even cancel the trust and remove or substitute property as long as he or she is alive.

An *Irrevocable Trust* means exactly that; it is irrevocable and cannot be changed once it is established. Also, property assigned to the trust cannot be recovered by the trustor, who is bound by the terms of his trust.

Can I draft my own trust?

Will and trust "kits" are available in most bookstores today. These purport to explain how to draft your own will or simple trust. Although it is legal for a layman to draft a holographic will or trust, I personally don't advise it. After your death, it's too late to change the will or trust if it doesn't pass the test. As the old saying goes, you can be "penny wise and pound foolish."

With so many restrictions attached to it, are there any benefits to creating an Irrevocable Trust?

At first glance, the *Revocable Trust* seems most desirable, since it can be changed or terminated during your lifetime, and you can recover any property you put into it. (At your death the trust becomes irrevocable.) Furthermore, you can name yourself as trustee or co-trustee, which allows you to maintain control of your assets and avoid trustee fees.

But in exchange for these benefits there is a major drawback. The assets of the *Revocable Trust* are included in the estate of the trustor at his or her death. This means they're subject to possible estate taxes.

In contrast, an *Irrevocable Trust* can provide significant tax savings. One example is the life insurance trust already discussed above. Another example involves using an irrevocable trust to hold gifts made under the *Annual Gift Tax Exclusion*. A couple could set up the trust for their children and give $10,000 per child per year to that trust under the *Annual Gift Tax Exclusion*. If both spouses consented to the gift, they could give up to $20,000 per child per year. If they had three children and a large estate, they might choose to give up to $60,000 per year and still avoid gift taxes.

Assets given to an *Irrevocable Trust* are excluded from the trustor's estate. All appreciation on the assets is also outside the estate. So, over a long period of time the trust value could double or triple through investment earnings and none of that would be subject to estate tax.

Since assets in an *Irrevocable Trust* can be excluded from my estate, may I use the trust as an asset protection vehicle in cases of major liability?

Yes. For example, suppose a father establishes an irrevocable trust for the purpose of educating his children. If the father became the target of a major lawsuit, any assets he placed beforehand in the *Irrevocable Trust* would be protected. So he could at least ensure that his children would be educated.

Assets placed in an *Irrevocable Trust* would also be protected in the case of a major creditor judgment, which would have the same devastating impact as a major lawsuit.

For persons with an extreme degree of liability, the *Irrevocable Trust* is a vital part of good planning. But it may also benefit people who don't expect to be the target of a major lawsuit. For example, a man who owns a small plumbing company could be sued for millions above his company's insurance limits if one of his employees had an accident while drinking and driving a company truck. If the owner has an *Irrevocable Trust,* he can take comfort in the fact that some assets will be protected.

37

Such planning is prudent in light of the fact that unforeseen events can strike anyone, regardless of who that person is, where he or she lives, or what business he or she is in.

Don operated a small import/export business specializing in office decorations. He used products from many of the developing countries that were highly promoted by the U.S. Government, including window coverings such as drapes and blinds.

Don made a particularly large sale of window blinds to a national company that required a fireproofing guarantee to meet the local fire codes for office buildings. He contacted the government representatives in the country of one of his suppliers and gave them the details he had been given. Within a week the certification came back along with the reports from the testing laboratory.

Based on this data, the company purchased nearly $125,000 in window coverings, netting Don a $45,000 profit—his largest ever.

A few months later one of the office buildings sustained a fire, during which the window coverings flashed and spread the flames. Several people were injured and filed lawsuits for several million dollars against the company that owned the building.

The office company had some of the window coverings tested and found that not only did they fail the fireproofing requirements, but they also put off toxic fumes when they flamed. As a result, the company filed suit against Don for $25 million.

In court Don showed evidence that he had relied on the data supplied by the foreign government agency representing the manufacturer, just as the office building owner had. The official response from the government agency was that the company was no longer in business and that they refused all responsibility.

Don lost the lawsuit and was assigned damages of more than $15 million. His liability insurance paid the $500,000 it was liable for, and the remainder was assessed against Don's company, which was forced into involuntary bankruptcy.

One of my main concerns in planning my estate is privacy. If I make a will, anyone can read the terms of that will at the courthouse; but there are some things I don't want to make public. Is there any way to keep my affairs more private?

Unlike wills, *Living Trusts* are "private" documents and, as such, do not require probate.

As a result, the terms of the trust won't be available for the public to read. To some people this may be no concern at all, but to others the level of privacy created by the trust is important enough to justify the cost.

In contrast, wills are available for reading in public places, such as the local courthouse. Wills can be written so that they don't reveal a lot about the size of a person's estate and what the assets consist of. But a person reading the will might still be able to determine certain facts about the estate, such as where the assets are assigned.

With a trust, however, the public at large has no right to inspect the trust document or inquire about the assets of the trust. Another benefit of the *Living Trust* being a private document is that assets held in the trust are not subject to probate costs or time delays.

Since a *Testamentary Trust* is usually created within a will, the assets in a *Testamentary Trust* will be subject to probate costs.

Probate costs can be very high in some states, making the cost of a trust worthwhile. In other states, however, the cost of probate may not be a key factor in establishing a trust. In that situation, establishment of a trust would depend on other factors, including a person's individual needs and circumstances.

Suppose I forget to include a few assets in my *Living Trust*. Will those assets still have to go through probate?

Yes. That's why you should have a *Pour Over Will* even if you plan to put all your assets into a *Living Trust*. For example, you may forget about certain assets and therefore neglect to put them in your trust. Or you may acquire assets later outside the trust and never get around to putting them in the trust.

The *Pour Over Will* provides that assets covered by the will when you die are to be transferred to the trust. Of course, because this outside property is covered by the will, it will still have to go through probate.

I own property in another state. Can I place that property in my Living Trust and avoid probate in that state as well?

Another situation in which trusts can be valuable is where a person owns property outside his state of residence. This involves *Ancillary Jurisdiction*, which can result in separate probate proceedings—one in your own state and other proceedings in the state or states where you may have had a vacation home or other property.

Ancillary Jurisdiction can be very expensive, requiring separate attorneys in each of the states where you own property. But if all your property is in a trust, you can avoid problems with *Ancillary Jurisdiction* and also reduce the cost of transferring assets to your heirs at death.

What happens if I become disabled or incapacitated and my assets are in a trust?

Actually, a trust would be one of the best places to have your assets in this situation. One of the most valuable uses of a trust is as a management vehicle for people who may not be able to manage their assets themselves. This is particularly true in the case of a person who has become disabled or incapacitated.

That's why an elderly person may wish to set up a trust now in the event that he becomes unable to manage his financial affairs. When the trust is established, a key decision must be made: who will serve as trustee. Like the executor, the trustee could be a spouse, relative, attorney, CPA, or the trust company of a bank.

The primary responsibility of the trustee is to carry out the terms of the trust. Among other things, the trustee might also be responsible for investing the trust assets and making distributions to the beneficiaries of the trust.

SECTION VI
The Trustee

What type of person is required to serve as trustee?

Unlike the duties of an executor, which are over once the administration of the estate is settled, the trustee's duties can last for a much longer term. A trust is normally meant to handle and disperse assets for a long period of time and requires periodic accounting and tax reports.

Thus, naming a trustee is somewhat more complicated and should be done after careful evaluation of the skills and experience necessary. For example, a widow with a spendthrift son might choose to place his inheritance in a trust instead of leaving it all to him in her will.

In this case, she would want to choose a trustee who could work with the beneficiary. At the same time, this individual would need to be firm enough to enforce the guidelines established by the widow for use of the trust assets. These guidelines might restrict use of the assets to things such as starting a business, educational expenses, or buying a house.

In the case of a *Living Trust*, the trustor can often serve as trustee. But the degree of control that person exercises can affect the taxable status of the trust assets. In the case of a testamentary trust, since it is created upon the death of the trustor, someone else must serve as trustee.

Trustees can be empowered to buy and sell trust assets and transact any business necessary in the name of the trust. The powers of the trustee should be spelled out in the trust document. Co-trustees can be named, and it is often desirable to appoint successor trustees. It may be a good idea to name a professional trustee as the final successor trustee in the event that none of your other trustees is able to serve.

SECTION VII
Types of Trusts

I'm looking for a way to lay aside money for my child's college education. Are there any trusts designed specifically for this purpose?

There are numerous types of trusts to fit a variety of needs. Detailing every one in this book would take more space than is available, but in order to get an idea of the different jobs that trusts can perform, a few examples are listed below.

2503 (c) TRUST

One of the most common needs for a trust is setting aside funds for your children's education, and the *2503(c) Trust* is often used for this purpose. The trust is named after the section of the Tax Code that authorizes it.

The trustor can make periodic gifts to the trust that are gift-tax free under the annual exclusion provisions of the Tax Code. And when the trust beneficiaries reach college age, the trustee disburses money to cover education costs.

FAMILY TRUSTS AND MARITAL TRUSTS

To understand how the *Family Trust* works, it is necessary to review two estate tax exemptions already discussed.

The first exemption is the *Unlimited Marital Deduction*, which exempts all property left to a spouse. The second is the *Unified Credit*, which exempts up to $600,000 left to children or someone other than a spouse. These exemptions can be used in conjunction with a *Family Trust* and a *Marital Trust* to produce significant tax savings.

For example, assume that an individual has an estate worth $1.2 million. When he dies, half of his estate ($600,000) goes into a *Marital Trust* for his wife. This amount is tax exempt under the *Unlimited Marital Deduction*. The other half of his estate (another $600,000) goes into a *Family Trust* for his children. This amount is also tax exempt under the *Unified Credit.*

The surviving spouse receives an income from both trusts during her lifetime. When she dies, the proceeds of the *Marital Trust* can be left to the children without incurring any tax. As far as the *Family Trust* is concerned, it has already been designated for the children.

Qualified Terminable Interest Property Trust (QTIP)

Like the *Marital Trust,* a *QTIP* trust can be used to leave money to a spouse. However, it does not allow the surviving spouse to leave the money to anyone else.

This can be useful in cases where the trustor or the surviving spouse has children from a prior marriage. After the death of the surviving spouse, the money from the *Qtip* trust is distributed according to the provisions of the trust. The *QTIP* trust is a testamentary trust that qualifies for the *Unlimited Marital Deduction.*

Irrevocable Life Insurance Trust

This trust is designed to keep life insurance proceeds from being subject to estate taxes.

The trust owns life insurance on the insured, and at the death of the insured, the insurance proceeds are paid to the trust for the benefit of the trust beneficiaries, typically the surviving spouse and children of the insured.

CHARITABLE REMAINDER TRUST

The *Charitable Remainder Trust* allows an individual to make a charitable gift in trust while reserving a right to income from the trust for a certain number of years or for life. When the individual dies, the life income interest terminates and the property remaining in the trust goes to the designated charities.

SECTION VIII

Stewardship and After-Death Bequests

I want to be the best possible steward of the resources God has entrusted to me, even after I'm gone. Is there a way to continue giving to the Lord's work after my death?

As stated earlier, all property is God's, and we are responsible for how we manage it. That responsibility doesn't end at death. As good stewards of what He has entrusted to us, we should consider what will happen to our property when we're no longer here. As a result, we may want a portion of our property to go to the Lord's work. But this won't happen unless we make a will. Be sure that if the state distributes your assets, none of it will go to a church, missionary, or ministry.

A number of ministries in this country, particularly large ones, have departments with attorneys who will assist you with the preparation of a will—*if you are planning to leave a portion of your estate to one of these ministries.* Generally, these legal services are free.

For some people, leaving money to a Christian organization may not be possible due to limited funds. The spouse and children may require all the family's assets to survive. But that could change if the entire family was killed in an accident.

In that case, you could have a provision in your will that says, "If my spouse and children don't survive me, I would like to have my estate, or a percentage of my estate, go to charitable institutions." Otherwise, your estate might go out to relatives who don't really need it, or to relatives you don't know very well.

I'm past retirement age and have the money to make some large charitable gifts. But I'm thinking about delaying those gifts and making them through my will in the form of an after-death bequest. Which option is better?

Much has been said in Christian circles about making bequests to the Lord's work upon one's death. For those expecting to die prematurely this is a good idea. But it is far better to *"do your givin' while you're livin', so you're knowin' where it's goin',"* as someone once said.

Ministries come and go, usually as the leaders come and go. A ministry that might be entirely sound and viable during your career years may go sour as the founder(s) passes on.

Thus, it is far better to give what you can to help such a ministry in its growth years than to wait until your death. Nevertheless, to have a plan in the event of your untimely death is both logical and biblical.

Too often, well-endowed organizations become complacent, and complacency breeds liberalism. A look at any of the well-heeled universities in the Northeast will verify this observation.

A look at most denominations that have been around a hundred years or more will also confirm this tendency. Many saints of the past would probably choke at how their endowments are now being used to promote every anti-Christian idea from abortion to homosexuality.

Remember, only God is wise enough to see the future. Do your giving while you are still around to see how it is used. "The generous man will be prosperous, and he who waters will Himself be watered" (Proverbs 11:25).

I have money that I'd like to leave to a charitable organization, but I need the income from that money while I'm living. I could leave the money through my will, but I'd like the satisfaction of giving it now. Is there a giving option that fits my needs?

There are a number of trust options for leaving a portion of your estate to the Lord's work and, at the same time, receiving income from the trust. You also receive an income tax deduction. Some of these trusts are described as follows.

CHARITABLE REMAINDER ANNUITY TRUST

Under the terms of this trust, you donate assets to a charity. Those assets are put into a trust, and you receive payments from the trust for up to twenty years or for life. At the end of this period, any assets left in the trust go to the charity. Your income payments must be made at least once a year and be no less than 5 percent of the initial fair market value of the trust property.

CHARITABLE REMAINDER UNITRUST

This trust is similar to the *Charitable Remainder Annuity Trust*, except that the size of the payment to the non-charitable beneficiaries (typically the trustor or members of his family) is set each year and rises or falls as the trust value rises or falls. Both types of charitable remainder trusts are designed to leave significant property to charitable organizations after the income interests terminate.

CHARITABLE LEAD TRUST

The *Charitable Lead Trust* works differently from the *Charitable Remainder Annuity Trust* or *Unitrust*. It makes income payments to the charity instead of you, and at the end of the income period, the remainder of the property goes to non-charitable beneficiaries (typically children of the trustor) instead of going to the charity.

SECTION IX
<u>Being Prepared</u>

Outside of making a will or trust, is there anything else I can do to make the settling of my estate a lot easier?

Even if you've already made a will and, if necessary, set up a trust, there are other steps you can take to improve the planning of your estate. One of the most important is making a list of where your important papers are and things to do in the event of your death. This will benefit your loved ones by eliminating a lot of confusion, which only adds to the emotional strain of losing a loved one. You may also wish to consult with your heirs before your death to determine which of your personal belongings they'd like to have. A few guidelines for dividing up these belongings are listed below.

MAKING A LIST OF INSTRUCTIONS

Losing a spouse can be such an emotional strain that trying to remember all the duties required to settle an estate can be difficult, if not impossible. For that reason, it's important to make a list of instructions and things to do in the event of your death.

What you put on *your* list depends on individual circumstances, but the purpose of the list is to assist your spouse and others involved with the settling of your estate. This includes having everything organized and knowing the location of important documents. Some common duties involved with settling an estate are listed below.

- *Death Certificate*—Obtain certified copies of the death certificate to file life insurance claims, apply for Social Security, settle banking and legal matters, and transfer titles to property recorded in the name of your spouse.
- *Life Insurance*—Locate all life insurance policies, including any life benefits that may be with your health insurance policy and any credit life benefit on outstanding

loans. Write each company and request a claims form and information on any requirements needed to process the claim.

- *Social Security*—Contact the Social Security office. They will give you the information over the phone or provide a pamphlet that explains your benefits and the requirements for filing a claim.
- *Veteran's Benefits*—If the spouse was a veteran, contact the Veteran's Administration for information on any benefits available to surviving spouses and dependent children.
- *Convert Titles*—Titles to properties owned jointly with rights of survivorship will need to be converted to the surviving joint tenant.
- *Bills*—Organize your bills according to due date, so that you don't fall behind on payments.
- *Important Documents*—Search for all important documents, including insurance policies, business agreements, bank books, loan agreements, securities, deeds, tax records, automobile titles, and birth and marriage certificates.

PREPARING FOR DIVISION OF ASSETS

If you're planning to divide personal belongings evenly between your children, you may want to consider having your assets appraised by a qualified appraiser.

If appropriate, you might ask each child if they desire any particular photographs and items of jewelry, artwork, and furniture. A properly prepared will and list of instructions can help provide for the proper division of assets.

SECTION X
Supplemental Income

How can I supplement my *Survivor's Benefits* to provide an adequate income if my spouse dies?

One of the most important considerations in being prepared for the death of a spouse is life insurance. It can be a valuable asset for widows or widowers who must suddenly bear the entire burden once shared by two people.

The amount of life insurance a family needs depends on many variables, such as family income, the ages of the children, the ability of the wife to earn an income, Social Security status, standard of living, and outstanding debts. The requirements will then have to be weighed against your budget. If the budget dollars are limited, it will be necessary to get as much insurance as possible for the available dollar.

In order to determine your insurance needs, you'll want to consider the following:

- **Present income per year**—How much income is being provided by the breadwinner of the family? The goal is to provide for the family so that they may continue the same living standard they enjoy under this income.
- **Payments no longer required**—Family expenses should drop as a result of the death of the breadwinner. For example, a second car may no longer be required; less income (or different income) will mean less taxes; activities or hobbies would not be an expense; investments or savings may be reduced or stopped.
- **Income available**—The breadwinner's death may initiate income from other sources, such as Social Security, retirement plans, investments, and annuities. The income-earning potential of a wife is a definite asset to the family, as illustrated by the preceding story. Ages of the children are a factor here. A minimum insurance program should provide time for obtaining or sharpening job skills if necessary.

- **Additional income required to support the family**—The income presently being earned less the payments no longer required and less the income available results in the income that needs to be supplied in order for the family to continue living on the same level enjoyed through the income of the husband.
- **Insurance required to provide needed income**—If provision could be made in an "ideal" manner, the insurance money invested at 10 percent would return the needed amount of income to the family. To find the required amount of insurance, multiply the income required to support the family by ten.

    Example: $7,000 additional income is required to support the family; $7,000 X 10 = $70,000. If you invest $70,000 in insurance at 10 percent, it would provide the needed funds.
- **Lump sum requirements**—In addition to the insurance required to produce the regular sustained income, lump sums may be required for specific purposes, such as a college education. Those needs should be determined and added to the total amount of insurance.

Are funds needed to pay off the home mortgage? This should be discussed as a part of the family plan. If mortgage payments are being made under the existing income, then this could be continued under the sustained income provision.

- **Assets available**—Determine the assets that are available for family provision. Subtract this amount from the desired amount of insurance. Equity in a home can be counted as an asset only if the survivors plan to sell it.
- **Total insurance needed**—The total tells how much insurance is needed. This must be balanced against how much can be spent for insurance. If the insurance dollars are limited, it will be necessary to get as close to the plan as possible with those dollars. Term insurance, with its lower initial premiums, probably offers the best opportunity for adequate provision with fewest dollars. The plan should also include instructions for how the insurance money is to be used.

SECTION XI
<u>Living Wills</u>

I've already made a will that explains how I want my estate to be settled. But a friend is telling me I also need a "Living Will." Is this really necessary, since I already have a will?

If you have a will or trust, you probably feel assured that your estate will be settled easily when you die. After all, you've established guidelines to eliminate possible confusion. But instead of dying, you could spend years in a hospital bed, suspended at some point between life and death.

In the case of serious, irreversible brain damage, your body might require the help of machines to continue functioning. These animated functions would be the only signs of life while you were held in limbo, unaware of your surroundings and unable to manage your affairs.

If all your estate plans were set to begin at death, your assets would also be in limbo while doctors, relatives, and perhaps even the courts debated about removing your life-support systems.

Situations like this are becoming more and more possible in this age of high-tech medicine, with its life-prolonging techniques. However, a new federal law called the *Patient Self-Determination Act* is aimed at dealing with these situations before they happen.

Effective December 1, 1991, the act requires all hospitals, nursing homes, and other facilities receiving *Medicaid or Medicare* funds to inform adult patients of their right to complete an "advance directive," which is a legal document allowing the patient to specify his or her choices about medical care.

One type of advance directive is the *Living Will*, which is recognized in most states. It can be used to request that life-prolonging techniques be withheld or withdrawn in the event of a situation like that described above.

To some, this represents the right of self-determination but, to others, it is man's attempt to make a decision reserved only for God. As would be expected, Christians and right-to-die advocates are on opposite sides of the fence. But there is a division over the issue even in the pro-life and evangelical communities.

At the heart of the debate is the question of how far to go in preserving life, even if the patient has no hope of recovery. This question also has doctors taking sides. For example, one doctor's association said treatment should be continued only as long as there's a chance for improvement. Another said treatment should be continued regardless of the patient's condition.

Thus, your doctor may not share your beliefs concerning life-prolonging treatment. That's why it's wise to discuss the issue with him or her before making a *Living Will*.

What are the guidelines for establishing a *Living Will*?

You should also contact your state health department or department on aging, because requirements for *Living Wills* vary from one state to another. And if you move to another state or spend a lot of time there, it's a good idea to create a *Living Will* for that state.

When completed, your *Living Will* should name someone you trust who can speak for you and, if necessary, defend your choice of medical treatment in court. This individual is called a *Proxy*, and in the same way that you name alternate executors and trustees, you should name an alternate *proxy* as well.

Sign your *Living Will* before two witnesses—other than relatives or *Proxies*—but give *Proxies* and family members a copy of the will. Your doctor should also receive a copy. Once your *Living Will* is completed, it's a good idea to initial and date it at least once a year.

As already noted, a *Living Will* can be used to express your desire not to be kept on life support systems. But you can also use it to request that life support be continued.

I understand that *Living Wills* only cover terminal conditions. What about some other condition that leaves me unable to manage my affairs?

Depending on the state in which you live, you may be able to execute a *Durable Power of Attorney for Health*

Care. This is a document that allows you to appoint an agent (typically a spouse) to make health care decisions for you in the event you are not able to make those decisions yourself.

Unlike a *Living Will*, which only covers a terminal condition, the *Durable Power of Attorney for Health Care* covers a broad range of health care problems. It is actually required in some states as a supplement to *Living Wills.*

All states will allow you to execute a *General Power of Attorney*, in which you can appoint someone to handle your business if you become incapacitated. Even if your state doesn't have a *Health Care Power of Attorney*, most legal scholars agree that *General Power of Attorney* laws are broad enough to include health care decisions.

Are there any specific items I need to cover in a *Living Will* or other type of health care planning vehicle?

Regardless of what plans you make, you need to be as specific as possible. For example, you might become comatose or vegetative and unable to eat by mouth. To keep you alive, a feeding tube could be surgically inserted into your stomach.

If you would not be opposed to tube feeding, you need to affirm that in your *Living Will*. Several states already have *Living Will* statutes that say you can't refuse tube feeding. But in the opinion of many state courts, you can still reject it even if a statute says you can't.

Other life-prolonging treatments that you may want to cover in your *Living Will* include respirators, kidney dialysis machines, and ventilators. Make your instructions as clear as possible. Persons who don't want to remain on life support indefinitely may place a time limit on how long they would want to continue in a comatose or vegetative state.

If family members are left with this decision, it can be emotionally devastating, and there may be disagreement. That's why you need to state your desires beforehand.

The issue of life support is something I hope my family never has to face. But if it arises, what questions might confront them?

Dealing with a loved one in a comatose or vegetative state involves some of the most difficult questions that a family could possibly encounter: "Will the patient recover?" "Is he in pain?" "How far is he from death?" "Will his condition remain unchanged for perhaps thirty years?"

The answers are often surprising, as in the case of a Presbyterian minister whose wife suffered from a brain hemorrhage and fell into a vegetative state. She was placed on a respirator, and doctors said her condition could last indefinitely.

In the meantime, her family suffered the emotional pain of seeing her in that condition. Her husband went to court to have the respirator removed, but the judged stayed his decision. Just six days later, the woman regained consciousness.

Another story involves an eighty-year-old woman who had opposed life-prolonging treatment before she suffered a cerebral hemorrhage and fell into a coma. After twelve days, her family decided to remove her feeding tube, but unexpectedly, she also regained consciousness.

One of the most highly publicized "right-to-die" cases involved Nancy Cruzan, a thirty-two-year-old woman who had been in a persistent vegetative state for seven years following a car accident. Facing the prospect that she could go on in that condition for thirty more years, Nancy's parents wanted to have her food and water tubes removed.

The case went all the way to the U.S. Supreme Court, but in June 1990 the court denied the Cruzans' request, noting there was no "clear and convincing" evidence that Nancy would have supported her parent's decision.

Even though the court failed to identify a "right to die" in the Constitution, it did give some legislative freedom on the issue to the states. And for the first time, it recognized a "constitutionally protected liberty interest in refusing unwanted medical treatment."

Ironically, the Cruzans' lawyers had argued that Nancy's liberty was being violated because a feeding tube had been surgically inserted into her stomach and she was being force-fed.

That brings up some difficult considerations associated with *Living Wills*:

1. At what point is man usurping God's authority to determine who lives and who dies? Some would say that point is reached when life support systems are removed. But

what about patients who have been kept alive for years in a vegetative state with no hope of recovery? If they would die without life support, are doctors also usurping God's authority by continuing their body functions?

2. Should families be concerned about the devastating financial impact of continuing life support for years and years? One argument for making a *Living Will* is that it saves family members from suffering through this financial nightmare. However, others argue that the value of human life does not depend on its quality or its cost.

3. If someone has suffered irreversible brain damage and has no awareness of his or her surroundings, does he or she reap any benefits from being kept alive for years in that condition?

4. Is it less humane to remove food and water tubes than to shut off a respirator or other type of life support system? As already stated, some states have laws prohibiting the removal of food and water tubes. If the patient requires no other form of life support, the only means of dying is starvation, which could take up to two weeks. The pain of hunger is a

sight that has always touched Americans, as in the Ethiopian famine several years ago. But that pain would be greatly multiplied if a loved one were involved.

It is at this point that euthanasia, the most critical issue associated with *Living Wills*, arises. For example, consider the case of a patient who required no life support except food and water tubes. Because removal of the tubes would cause starvation, and death might require two weeks, some would support giving the patient a lethal injection instead.

In a 1990 survey, individuals were asked what choices they would make in the case of an unconscious, terminally ill patient who had left instructions in a *Living Will*. Over 80 percent said the doctor should be allowed to remove life-support systems. However, 57 percent went as far as saying that the doctor should be allowed to give the patient a lethal injection or lethal pills.

Some fear that if right-to-die measures become too lax, the result will be involuntary euthanasia, in which death is forced upon those people who are considered a "burden" to society.

Living Wills

As a Christian, you need to consider all the questions and issues associated with *Living Wills*. Some twenty-one million Americans die each year, and most of those deaths occur in hospitals or nursing homes, where life-prolonging techniques are often used. Without instructions from you, doctors in these institutions and members of your family must debate this difficult issue. If for no other reason, you should state your wishes in advance.

SECTION XII
Professional Advisors

W hat are the advantages of using a professional advisor to help me plan my estate?

Depending on the size of your estate, you may wish to consult an expert in the field of financial and/or estate planning. By working with an expert advisor, you can begin to define your long-term goals and what is required to achieve them. These goals may include educating your children or having sufficient resources for retirement. But if you're going to use the services of a financial advisor, make sure that individual is qualified, because it's *your* money at stake.

What guidelines should I follow in choosing an advisor?

There are all sorts of financial advisors, ranging from those who do more harm than good to those who really help you achieve your goals. Although there is no guaranteed formula for choosing the best advisor, there are some guidelines you can follow in making your decision.

Like other professions, financial planning has professional designations. These include the *Certified Financial Planner (CFP)* and the *Chartered Financial Consultant (ChFC)*. Although designations don't guarantee the competency of the advisor, they do show that he or she has gone through a disciplined course of study and completed the requirements of that course, including examinations. These designations represent what might be called a first level of screening.

Certified Public Accountants (CPAs) and attorneys who are working in the financial planning area can also be of great benefit, especially when tax issues are involved. But outside of professional designations, it also helps to obtain references.

You should also check with two or three advisors. Get an idea of their temperament and philosophy, and see if you feel comfortable talking to them about your finances and your goals. Most of all, be sure you feel comfortable with the advice they give.

I realize that caution should always be used in choosing an investment. But what about investing with an advisor? Don't they know all the best investments?

Unfortunately, that's not always the case. Fraudulent practices by investment advisors is believed to cost investors half a billion dollars each year.

Dealing with a financial advisor is a relationship based on trust, which is developed over time. Because your life savings may be involved, don't act too hastily in choosing an advisor and especially in risking your funds.

CFC gratefully acknowledges the assistance of George M. Hiller in the preparation of this booklet. Mr. Hiller is head of the George M. Hiller Companies in Atlanta. He holds a J. D. (Doctor of Laws) degree, an L L. M. (Master of Laws) degree, and a master's degree in business administration. Mr. Hiller has been admitted to the Registry of Financial Planning Practitioners and is a Certified Financial Planner (CFP). In addition to assisting with this booklet, he has been quoted in articles for major publications such as *Money* magazine and *USA Today.*

Christian
Financial
Concepts

Teaching God's Principles of Handling Money

Larry Burkett, founder and president of Christian Financial Concepts, is the best-selling author of more than a dozen books on business and personal finances. He also hosts two radio programs broadcast on hundreds of stations worldwide.

Larry holds degrees in marketing and finance, and for several years served as a manager in the space program at Cape Canaveral, Florida. He also has been vice-president of an electronics manufacturing firm. Larry's education, business experience, and solid understanding of God's Word enable him to give practical, Bible-based financial counsel to families, churches, and businesses.

Founded in 1976, Christian Financial Concepts is a nonprofit, nondenominational ministry dedicated to helping God's people gain a clear understanding of how to manage their money according to scriptural principles. Although practical assistance is provided on many levels, the purpose of CFC is simply *to bring glory to God by freeing His people from financial bondage so that they may serve Him to their utmost.*

One major avenue of ministry involves the training of volunteers in budget and debt counseling and linking them with financially troubled families and individuals through a nationwide referral network. CFC also provides financial management seminars and workshops for churches and other groups.

(Formats available include audio, video, video with moderator, and live instruction.) A full line of printed and audio-visual materials related to money management is available through CFC's materials department (1-800-722-1976).

Career Pathways, another outreach of Christian Financial Concepts, helps teenagers and adults find their occupational calling. The Career Pathways "Testing Package" gauges a person's work priorities, skills, vocational interests, and personality. Reports in each of these areas define a person's strengths, weaknesses, and unique, God-given pattern for work.

For further information about the ministry of Christian Financial Concepts, write to:

Christian Financial Concepts
P.O. Box 2377
Gainesville, Georgia 30503-2377

Other Materials by Larry Burkett:

Books in this series:

Financial Freedom
Sound Investments
Major Purchases
Insurance Plans
Giving and Tithing
Personal Finances
Surviving the 90's Economy
Your Financial Future
The Financial Sampler

Other Books:

Debt-Free Living
The Financial Planning Workbook
How to Manage Your Money
Your Finances in Changing Times
The Coming Economic Earthquake

Videos:

Your Finances in Changing Times
Two Masters
How to Manage Your Money
The Financial Planning Workbook

Other Resources:

The Financial Planning Organizer
Debt-Free Living Cassette